*L*ENT *and* *E*ASTER *W*ISDOM

from

SAINT VINCENT DE PAUL

LENT and EASTER WISDOM

from
SAINT VINCENT
DE PAUL

Daily Scripture and Prayers Together
With Saint Vincent de Paul's Own Words

Compiled by John E. Rybolt, CM

Liguori
LIGUORI, MISSOURI

Imprimi Potest: Harry Grile, CSsR
Provincial, Denver Province, The Redemptorists

Published by Liguori Publications
Liguori, Missouri 63057

To order, call 800-325-9521
www.liguori.org

Introduction; prayers, adaptations, and compilation for Parts I and II; and Lenten and Easter Actions © 2012 John E. Rybolt, CM

Library of Congress Cataloging-in-Publication Data
Vincent de Paul, Saint, 1581-1660.
    [Selections. English. 2012]
    Lent and Easter wisdom from St. Vincent de Paul / [edited by] John E. Rybolt. —1st ed.
        p. cm.
    1. Lent—Prayers and devotions. 2. Easter—Prayers and devotions. 3. Catholic Church—Prayers and devotions. I. Rybolt, John E. II. Title.
    BX2170.L4V56 2012
    242'.34—dc23
                                                                                        2012024296

p ISBN 978-0-7648-2011-3

e ISBN 978-0-7648-2321-3

Vincent de Paul quotations are from *Correspondence, conferences, documents* by Saint Vincent de Paul ; newly translated, edited, and annotated from the 1920 edition of Pierre Coste. Volume 11. http://via.library.depaul.edu/lcd/.

Compliant with *The Roman Missal,* third edition.

Liguori Publications, a nonprofit corporation, is an apostolate of The Redemptorists. To learn more about The Redemptorists, visit Redemptorists.com.

Printed in the United States of America

16 15 14 13 12 / 5 4 3 2 1
First Edition

Contents

Introduction

Saint Vincent de Paul (1580/81–1660) is commonly called the Saint or even Apostle of Charity. He became a priest at a very young age in search of a comfortable living but gradually abandoned this as he encountered the poor. For him, the poor, especially the most abandoned, were the surest avenue to reach the Lord. From his thirties he dedicated himself to their care.

In art, he is often depicted with children, but his true concentration was evangelization, particularly the poor. He founded two communities to carry on this work, the Congregation of the Mission (called Vincentians or Lazarists), and the Daughters of Charity. For them, he developed a new, even radical, style of life. The sisters were to dress in secular clothing and live an active apostolate. He strove to form the priests and brothers into contemplatives in action, just as he was.

We are fortunate to have much of his correspondence. Also valuable are his talks, or "conferences," given to both congregations. This book endeavors to present his thoughts in a way that can likewise lead to a deeper relationship with God, a better appreciation of one's own Christian life, and greater love for all, especially the poor.

The meditative texts used here are taken from conferences to his confreres. Vincent de Paul did not often reflect on Lent or Easter directly, but he was keenly aware of the greater issues of our life in

Christ, whose passion, death, and resurrection are celebrated at this season.

You can use this book in several ways. You might write your ideas or resolutions in a journal, or perhaps in the book on the days indicated. In rereading your notes later, you will find added strength in the inspirations you receive.

A Brief History of Lent

Most Catholics seem to be aware that the forty-day period before the feast of Easter—Lent, which comes from the Anglo-Saxon word lencten, meaning "spring"—is a time marked by particular rituals such as the reception of ashes on Ash Wednesday or the decision to give up french fries. Is Lent broader than just these practices that seem to be left over from another era?

In the first three centuries of Christian experience, preparation for the Easter feast usually covered a period of one or two days, perhaps a week at the most. Saint Irenaeus of Lyons (ca. AD 140–202) even speaks of a forty-hour preparation for Easter.

The first reference to Lent as a period of forty days' preparation occurs in the teachings of the First Council of Nicaea in AD 325. By the end of the fourth century, a Lenten period of forty days was established and accepted.

In its early development, Lent quickly became associated with the sacrament of baptism, since Easter was the great baptismal feast. Those who were preparing to be baptized participated in the season of Lent in preparation for the reception of the sacrament of baptism. Eventually, those who were already baptized considered it important to join these candidates preparing for baptism in their preparations for Easter. The customs and practices of Lent as we know them today soon took hold.

LENT AS A JOURNEY

Lent is often portrayed as a journey, from one point in time to another point in time. The concept of journey is obvious for those experiencing the Rite of Christian Initiation of Adults (RCIA), the program of baptismal preparation conducted in most parishes during the season of Lent.

But Lenten preparation is not limited to those who are preparing to be baptized and join the Church. For many Catholics, Lent is a journey that is measured from Ash Wednesday through Easter Sunday, but more accurately, Lent is measured from Ash Wednesday to the beginning of the period known as the Triduum.

Triduum begins with the Mass on Holy Thursday, continues through Good Friday, and concludes with the Easter Vigil on Holy Saturday. Triduum officially ends with the proclamation of the Exsultet, "Rejoice, O Heavenly Powers," during the Mass of Holy Saturday.

By whatever yardstick the journey is measured, it is not only the time that is important but the essential experiences of the journey that are necessary for a full appreciation of what is being celebrated.

The Lenten journey is also a process of spiritual growth and, as such, presumes movement from one state of being to another. For example, some people may find themselves troubled and anxious at the beginning of Lent as a result of a life choice or an unanswered question, and, at the end of Lent, they may fully expect a sense of conversion, a sense of peace, or perhaps simply understanding and acceptance. Therefore, Lent is a movement from one point of view to another or, perhaps, from one interpretation of life to a different one.

Scripture, psalms, prayers, rituals, practices, and penance are the components of the Lenten journey. Each component, tried and tested by years of tradition, is one of the "engines" that drives the season and which brings the weary spiritual traveler to the joys of Easter.

PENITENTIAL NATURE OF LENT

A popular understanding of Lent is that it is a penitential period of time during which people attempt to become more sensitive to the role of sin in their lives. Lenten sermons will speak of personal sin, coming to an awareness of the sins of others and the effect such sin might have, and the sin that can be found within our larger society and culture. Awareness of sin, however, is balanced by an emphasis on the love and acceptance that God still has for humanity, despite the sinful condition in which we still find ourselves.

The practice of meditation of the Passion of the Lord, his suffering and his death, is also seen as part of the penitential experience of Lent. There is also a traditional concern for the reception of the sacrament of reconciliation during Lent. Originally, the sacrament of reconciliation was celebrated before Lent began. The penance was imposed on Ash Wednesday and performed during the entire forty-day period.

SUMMONS TO PENITENTIAL LIVING

"Jesus came to Galilee, proclaiming the good news of God, and saying, 'The time is fulfilled, and the kingdom of God has come near; repent, and believe in the good news'" (Mark 1:14–15). This call to conversion announces the solemn opening of Lent. Participants are marked with ashes, and the words, "Repent, and believe in the good news," are prayed. This blessing is understood as a personal acceptance of the desire to take on the life of penance for the sake of the gospel.

The example of Jesus in the desert for forty days—a time during which he fasted and prayed—is imitated. It is time to center attention on conversion. During Lent, the expectation is to examine our lives and, through the practice of prayer, fasting, and works of charity, seek to conform our lives to Christ's. For some, this conversion will be a turning from sin to grace. For others, it will be a gracious turning toward the mystery of God in Christ. Whatever the pattern chosen by a particular pilgrim for an observance of Lent, it is hoped that this book will provide a useful support in the effort.

PART I

READINGS for LENT

Ash Wednesday

Whole Burnt Offerings

*A*mong the sacrifices offered to God in the Old Law, holocaust [burnt] was the most excellent one because, in recognition of the sovereignty of God, the victim was burned and consumed entirely on the altars, without saving anything. Everything was reduced to dust and ashes for the glory of God. I think we could call those souls [the martyrs] victims of love—holocausts—since, without holding anything back for themselves, they are consumed and perish because of it.

"REPETITION OF PRAYER," CONFERENCE 129

BURNT OFFERING

If a person's offering is a burnt offering from the herd, the offering must be a male without blemish. The individual shall bring it to the entrance of the tent of meeting to find favor with the LORD, and shall lay a hand on the head of the burnt offering, so that it may be acceptable to make atonement for the one who offers it.

LEVITICUS 1:3–4

PRAYER

Lord God, strengthen me to offer the sacrifices you ask of me in daily life. May I embrace them and offer myself to you as a whole burnt offering. Take away any bitterness that I may experience as I face the demands of life. Give me your joy instead and a sense of your presence.

LENTEN ACTION

At the beginning of this Lent, think about the ashes you receive. Palms and other branches were consumed to produce them, and we receive them today on our foreheads as a sign of inner commitment to the Lord. You might also repeat the action during this season, burning a leaf or piece of paper, and viewing the consuming fire and ash as a reminder of your deepest gift of self to God.

Hold Fast Against Nature

*L*et's hold fast against our nature; for, if we give it an inch, it will take a mile. And we can rest assured that the measure of our progress in the spiritual life must be taken from the progress we're making in the virtue of mortification....

"MORTIFICATION," CONFERENCE 52

CRUCIFY THE FLESH

Now those who belong to Christ (Jesus) have crucified their flesh with its passions and desires. If we live in the Spirit, let us also follow the Spirit.

GALATIANS 5: 24–25

PRAYER

Lord Jesus, if I am to follow you, I must also put to death elements of my life that are not worthy of you, or of me as a member of your mystical body. Send me your strong Holy Spirit to lead and guide me in this Lenten purification.

LENTEN ACTION

Fasting today almost always refers to abstaining from food. It can also be seen as abstention from the "passions and desires" that lurk within everyone. Pray today about the meaning of fasting for you. What is it that your human nature wants that is ultimately against the teachings of the gospel? Take this as your guide for Lenten fasting.

Prisoners, the Poor and Abandoned

*A*re you aware that in the past there were popes engaged in the care of animals? Yes, in the times of the emperors who were persecuting the Church in its head and in its members, they used to arrest the popes and make them look after the lions, leopards, and other similar beasts that would serve as entertainment for those infidel princes and were like images of their cruelty; and the popes were the ones who took care of these animals.

"THOSE CONFINED AT ST. LAZARE," CONFERENCE 13

WHEN DID WE SEE YOU...?

"For I was hungry and you gave me food, I was thirsty and you gave me drink,...in prison and you visited me." Then the righteous will answer him and say, "Lord,...when did we see you ill or in prison, and visit you?" And the king will say to them in reply, "Amen, I say to you, whatever you did for one of these least brothers of mine, you did for me."

MATTHEW 25:35–40

PRAYER

God, you have graciously kept my life free of the violence and cruelty that afflicts so many in today's world. I call on your mercy toward those who are suffering unjustly, those without hope of release from mindless cruelty and oppression. Send them your light and good people to be with them and serve them. Help me to find ways to be of service, too.

LENTEN ACTION

The care of prisoners has always been a hallmark of Christian service, even though our brothers and sisters have suffered at the hands of Christian masters. Examine your heart in this Lenten season to see what you could do to relieve their sufferings, directly or indirectly. Prayer for them may be the only possibility, but support and concern expressed indirectly, through others, can also fulfill the Lord's command. Many opportunities exist to be of direct service. Ask for the Lord's inspiration to help you find the one that fits you best.

Proper Speech

*O*ne of the effects of prudence and wisdom is not only to speak well and to say good things, but also to say them at the right time so that they may be well received and beneficial to the persons to whom we speak. Our Lord gave the example of this on several occasions, especially when He was speaking to the Samaritan woman.

"PRUDENCE IN CONVERSATIONS," CONFERENCE 34B

THE SAMARITAN WOMAN

The Samaritan woman said to him, "How can you, a Jew, ask me, a Samaritan woman, for a drink?" (For Jews use nothing in common with Samaritans.) Jesus answered and said to her, "If you knew the gift of God and who is saying to you, 'Give me a drink,' you would have asked him and he would have given you living water."

JOHN 4:9–10

PRAYER

Lord, I know how difficult it is to control my speech, since these words flow at times from my lack of attention to others and too much attention to myself. May my words be more like the fountain of living water, to bring healing, and less like a destructive flame.

LENTEN ACTION

Lent is a time for renewed discipline. Today, pray in the morning about the important occasions when you will have to speak during the day, and plan to make them as graceful and healing as possible. In the evening, examine your conscience to review what happened. If you succeeded, praise God. If not, ask his pardon and light to know better how to speak as Jesus would.

Temptation

*O*ne of the surest signs that God has great plans for someone is
when He sends him distress upon distress and trouble upon
trouble. The real time to recognize the spiritual mettle of a soul is
the time of temptation and tribulation because the way we are during these trials is the way we usually are afterward.

"Patience," Conference 47a

The Temptation of Jesus

Filled with the holy Spirit, Jesus returned from the Jordan and was led by the Spirit into the desert for forty days, to be tempted by the devil. He ate nothing during those days, and when they were over he was hungry. The devil said to him, "If you are the Son of God, command this stone to become bread." Jesus answered him, "It is written, 'One does not live by bread alone.'"

Luke 4:1–4

Prayer

Lord Jesus, even you were tempted. I acknowledge my own temptations and falls. Help me not to be discouraged by the darkness I see in myself. Rather, may your light and truth guide me along the right paths in my life.

Lenten Action

As your Lenten observance begins, take time in prayer to see in what ways you are tempted to break your commitments to the Lord. Admit their presence in your life and write them down if you keep a journal. Coming to terms with your real self is a salutary way to face the discipline of Lent.

Reconciliation

*T*here are even many soldiers who come here, and one of them said to me a short time ago, "Monsieur, I'll soon have to go into certain situations, and I want to put myself in a good state beforehand; I have remorse of conscience, and, not knowing what might happen to me, I'm here to prepare myself for whatever God will want to ordain for me."

"RETREAT MINISTRY," CONFERENCE 9

THE PRODIGAL SON

His son said to him, "Father, I have sinned against heaven and against you; I no longer deserve to be called your son." But his father ordered his servants, "Quickly bring the finest robe and put it on him; put a ring on his finger and sandals on his feet. Take the fattened calf and slaughter it. Then let us celebrate with a feast, because this son of mine was dead, and has come to life again; he was lost, and has been found."

LUKE 15: 21–24

PRAYER

Lord Jesus, I hear the words of the compassionate Father directed to me: You were lost and have been found. Help me now to celebrate my return to your love in the sacrament of Reconciliation, and strengthen my love for the reconciliation you offer in so many other ways.

LENTEN ACTION

Lent is the most important time liturgically for the celebration of our reconciliation in Christ. Prepare for the sacrament seriously, with time for prayer, for reflection on the course of your life, and for peace in tasting the pardon offered you by a merciful Lord. Thank him for the grace of the sacrament.

Self-Denial

*H*ow many men are coming here from far and near on the inspiration of the Holy Spirit! But what a powerful grace is needed to lead men from all over to such a crucifixion, for a spiritual retreat aims to crucify the flesh, so we can say with the holy Apostle, "I am crucified to the world, and the world to me."

"RETREAT MINISTRY," CONFERENCE 12

CRUCIFIED TO THE WORLD

But may I never boast except in the cross of our Lord Jesus Christ, through which the world has been crucified to me, and I to the world. For neither does circumcision mean anything, nor does uncircumcision, but only a new creation. Peace and mercy be to all who follow this rule and to the Israel of God.

GALATIANS 6:14–16

PRAYER

Lord Jesus, if I am to follow you in my own life, I have to follow you in your passion and death to attain resurrection with you. Help me to see your loving guidance in all the problems and pains of my daily life. When my health is weak, let me see the cross there for me to embrace. When my plans come to nothing, let me grasp the disappointments as my share of your saving passion.

LENTEN ACTION

Many saints are pictured holding a small crucifix to meditate on its meaning. This contemplation of the crucified Jesus transformed their lives. Take some time during this Lent, not only today but often, to meditate on the cross in prayer. Let the love shown there take root in your heart and transform your spirit. Growth in love is always the goal of such a devotion.

Effective Love, in Service

*N*ow, it must be noted that love is divided into affective and effective love. Affective love is a certain outpouring from the one who loves to the loved one, or a pleasure and tender feeling one has for the thing loved, as a father has for his child, etc. Effective love consists in doing the things the loved person commands or desires.

"LOVE OF GOD," CONFERENCE 26

PURE RELIGION

But the one who peers into the perfect law of freedom and perseveres, and is not a hearer who forgets but a doer who acts, such a one shall be blessed in what he does. If anyone thinks he is religious and does not bridle his tongue but deceives his heart, his religion is vain. Religion that is pure and undefiled before God and the Father is this: to care for orphans and widows in their affliction and to keep oneself unstained by the world.

JAMES 1:25–27

PRAYER

God of the universe, you are love. For me to follow you more closely, I need to grow in love. May my love, then, be more than feeling but active and effective instead. At the end of Lent may I have grown in the practice of love in all aspects of my life.

LENTEN ACTION

Use a journal to keep track of your Lenten thoughts and inspirations. An important element will be to write down where, how, and in what circumstances you have practiced your love for God effectively, in action. This can reinforce growth in virtue and in mindfulness of others.

Despair Over Sins

M. Vincent told us not to be surprised to see ourselves in deplorable states of despair and to have horrible, abominable thoughts. All those states do not come from ourselves, but God permits them in order to test us....

"TRIALS AND ATTACHMENTS," CONFERENCE 89

TEARS FOR SINS

Now there was a sinful woman in the city who learned that he was at table in the house of the Pharisee. Bringing an alabaster flask of ointment, she stood behind him at his feet weeping and began to bathe his feet with her tears. Then she wiped them with her hair, kissed them, and anointed them with the ointment. When the Pharisee who had invited him saw this he said to himself, "If this man were a prophet, he would know who and what sort of woman this is who is touching him, that she is a sinner."

LUKE 7:37–39

PRAYER

Father, I blush when I think of the sins I have committed in my life. I often do not know why I turn away from your holy word, but I still do so. Help me now, in this Lent, to see myself as I am and to offer myself to you anew. Cleanse and purify me as only you know how.

LENTEN ACTION

If you have habits of thinking and acting that do not fulfill the gospel precepts, admit that they are present in your life. Offer yourself to God as you are, in your brokenness and weakness. Come back to this often during Lent and beg the Lord's healing. Everyone, even Jesus, was subject to temptations.

Fleeing Our Crosses

*W*oe betide the person who seeks his own satisfactions! Woe betide the person who flees from crosses, for he'll find such heavy ones that they'll overwhelm him!

"MORTIFICATION," CONFERENCE 53

CRUCIFIED WITH CHRIST

For through the law I died to the law, that I might live for God. I have been crucified with Christ; yet I live, no longer I, but Christ lives in me; insofar as I now live in the flesh, I live by faith in the Son of God who has loved me and given himself up for me.

GALATIANS 2:19–20

PRAYER

Lord Jesus, as I try to follow your way during Lent, I see the crosses of my daily life. May your sacraments strengthen me to embrace the way you set before me.

LENTEN ACTION

Take up again the crucifix you use for your daily devotions. Look at it and try to appreciate both the sufferings of our Lord but also those you face. It is much harder to embrace the crosses we are given than those of Jesus centuries ago. With calm and meditative prayer centered on the crucifix you can see the Lord's path spread out before you. Embrace it in faith and love.

Retreats

*Y*es, a well-made retreat is a total renewal: the man who has made one as it should be made passes into another state. He's no longer what he was; he becomes another man.

"THE EXCELLENCE OF SPIRITUAL RETREATS," CONFERENCE 77

A DESERT EXPERIENCE

The report about him spread all the more, and great crowds assembled to listen to him and to be cured of their ailments, but he would withdraw to deserted places to pray.

LUKE 5:15–16

PRAYER

Lord Jesus Christ, I wish to follow you as you withdrew to be alone and quiet in prayer. Give me the inspiration and guidance to know how to do so, and so be with you more intimately.

LENTEN ACTION

Have you had the experience of a retreat? Some days or even some hours away from the routine of ordinary life can be a great stimulus to prayer and conversion of life. Make plans to do this, either during this Lent or at some other time. Ask yourself how much activity you can put aside for some time so as to grow in your spiritual life.

DAY 12   SECOND SUNDAY OF LENT

Jesus and the Poor

I must not judge a poor peasant man or woman by their appearance or their apparent intelligence, especially since very often they scarcely have the expression or the mind of rational persons, so crude and vulgar they are. But turn the medal, and you will see by the light of faith that the Son of God, who willed to be poor, is represented to us by these poor people.

"THE SPIRIT OF FAITH," CONFERENCE 19

TRANSFIGURATION

After six days Jesus took Peter, James, and John and led them up a high mountain apart by themselves. And he was transfigured before them, and his clothes became dazzling white, such as no fuller on earth could bleach them. Then a cloud came, casting a shadow over them; then from the cloud came a voice, "This is my beloved Son. Listen to him."

MARK 9:2–3, 7

PRAYER

Lord, I would have been as overwhelmed as Peter, James, and John had I been present at your transfiguration. Give me the insight I need today to pierce the veil of flesh and see you living in the lives of my sisters and brothers, especially the poor. Give me the same vision of you in the sacramental signs that you so lavishly bestow on your Church.

LENTEN ACTION

The next time you pass poor people on the street or someone asking for help, remember that they were someone's children and that, even if their life has taken a bad turn, the Lord still loves them. Dig deeper into your thoughts and "turn the medal," as Saint Vincent urged, to see the poor Son of God there. A word, a smile, a gift would be an appropriate response to this transfiguration of the poor.

Conversion to the Faith

*R*emember another one in your prayers as well, a new convert—a very good one—from the so-called reformed religion; right now he's working and writing for the defense of the truth he has embraced, and by this means will be able to win over others. We thank God for this and entreat Him to increase His graces in him more and more.

"RETREAT MINISTRY," CONFERENCE 11

PAUL'S CONVERSION

And I was unknown personally to the churches of Judea that are in Christ; they only kept hearing that "the one who once was persecuting us is now preaching the faith he once tried to destroy." So they glorified God because of me.

GALATIANS 1:22–24

PRAYER

God, almighty Father, I praise and thank you for bringing me to the faith that your son, Jesus, preached to the world. Sometimes my faith is weak and hesitant, and I find that I am your follower in name only. During this Lenten season, reach into my heart and give me a renewed sense of your love for me. May I live out my faith fully and completely and share the Good News with others.

LENTEN ACTION

You recite the Nicene Creed at Mass and know the Apostles' Creed from years of practice. Each phrase was crafted by your ancestors in the faith to express their deepest commitments. Take some time to read these texts slowly and meditatively. Question yourself about each phrase and read and study what others have written about them. This is the faith of the Church so carefully handed on to catechumens during the Lenten season. Make it yours, too.

Stripping of Self

As for me, I know nothing more holy or more perfect than this resignation, when it leads to a total stripping of self and to genuine indifference with regard to all sorts of states in whatever way we're placed in them, sin excepted. So, let's hold fast to that, and ask God to grant us the grace to remain constantly in this state of indifference.

"CONFORMITY TO THE WILL OF GOD," CONFERENCE 27

THE POTTER

I went down to the potter's house and there he was, working at the wheel. Whenever the vessel of clay he was making turned out badly in his hand, he tried again, making another vessel of whatever sort he pleased. Then the word of the LORD came to me: Can I not do to you, house of Israel, as this potter has done?—oracle of the LORD. Indeed, like clay in the hand of the potter, so are you in my hand, house of Israel.

JEREMIAH 18:3–6

PRAYER

Lord Jesus, as I follow you during this Lent, I want to do your will for me in all things. Through my prayer, fasting, and almsgiving, mold me as clay into the person I should be. May I become the vessel you want me to be.

LENTEN ACTION

Be like the prophet and watch someone make something. Mold something yourself, like dough for bread. Then take the time to pray over the work of your hands and see in it a symbol of God working on you.

Service for Charity

*I*f, nevertheless, God allowed them to be reduced to the necessity of going to serve as priests in the villages to earn their living, or even if some of them were obliged to go to beg for their bread or to sleep under some bush, in ragged clothing and chilled to the bone, and someone should ask one of them, "Poor Priest of the Mission, what has reduced you to these straits?" what a happiness, Messieurs, to be able to reply, "It's charity!" How that poor priest would be esteemed before God and the angels!

"CHARITY," CONFERENCE 60

THE BOND OF PERFECTION

Put on then, as God's chosen ones, holy and beloved, heartfelt compassion, kindness, humility, gentleness, and patience, bearing with one another and forgiving one another, if one has a grievance against another; as the Lord has forgiven you, so must you also do. And over all these put on love, that is, the bond of perfection.

COLOSSIANS 3:12–14

PRAYER

Heavenly Father, the cares of daily life sometimes keep me from you. During these weeks of prayer, fasting, and almsgiving, inspire in me a deeper sense of charity toward others, even when it calls for genuine sacrifice from me. May you alone be my reward.

LENTEN ACTION

Almsgiving is the third traditional activity for Lent. Listen to the voice of God's spirit speaking in your heart about the charity you could undertake during this time of preparation for Easter.

Gift of the Eucharist

O Lord, be forever praised and thanked for having given me Your Flesh and Blood for food and drink! O my Savior, how can I thank You worthily for this!

"REPETITION OF PRAYER," CONFERENCE 119

COMMUNION WITH JESUS AND THE NEIGHBOR

The cup of blessing that we bless, is it not a participation in the blood of Christ? The bread that we break, is it not a participation in the body of Christ? Because the loaf of bread is one, we, though many, are one body, for we all partake of the one loaf.

1 CORINTHIANS 10:16–17

PRAYER

Lord Jesus, give me a renewed sense of your presence in the holy Eucharist. May my reception of the sacrament never become routine or ordinary, but rather an ever-deeper encounter with you. As I enter again into Communion with you, may I also be open to deeper relationships with my sisters and brothers, especially those in greatest need.

LENTEN ACTION

During this Lent, plan to attend the Eucharist more often than you normally do, even at some sacrifice of your personal time. Bring to these celebrations not only your own intentions, but those of others who are not present. Lift them up to the Lord in the confidence that his love is everlasting.

DAY 17 FRIDAY OF THE SECOND WEEK OF LENT

Conversion for All

G od uses whomever he pleases and any person who seems good to him to procure his glory....He can raise up children of Abraham from these stones. God is all-powerful and, if He chooses, He can use the hardness of this stone to soften the most hardened hearts and lead them to a holy conversion and penance.

"METHOD TO BE FOLLOWED IN PREACHING," CONFERENCE 133

FROM STONES TO CHILDREN

"Produce good fruits as evidence of your repentance; and do not begin to say to yourselves, 'We have Abraham as our father,' for I tell you, God can raise up children to Abraham from these stones. Even now the ax lies at the root of the trees. Therefore every tree that does not produce good fruit will be cut down and thrown into the fire." And the crowds asked him, "What then should we do?" He said to them in reply, "Whoever has two cloaks should share with the person who has none. And whoever has food should do likewise."

LUKE 3:8–11

PRAYER

Creator God, all things have their origin and growth in you. During this Lent, send me your word in holy Scripture and in the homilies I hear. May this word soften my heart and give me a deeper sense of your love for me. Strengthen me to spread this love, especially in acts of mercy toward those who most need it.

LENTEN ACTION

Vincent de Paul had a strong sense of the presence of God working in the world. Try to follow his example today by growing in his practical love for those around you: friends, family, and especially the poor you encounter. Ask yourself: Am I growing daily in love? If so, how does it show itself?

No One Is Perfect

*P*erfection doesn't consist in ecstasies but in doing the will of God. What is perfection? I think it means something in which nothing is lacking. Now, what man is so perfect that he lacks nothing, since no man is perfect and the most just man sins seven times a day?

"REPETITION OF PRAYER," CONFERENCE 143

CONSTANT FORGIVENESS

He said to his disciples, "Things that cause sin will inevitably occur, but woe to the person through whom they occur. It would be better for him if a millstone were put around his neck and he be thrown into the sea than for him to cause one of these little ones to sin. Be on your guard! If your brother sins, rebuke him; and if he repents, forgive him. And if he wrongs you seven times in one day and returns to you seven times saying, 'I am sorry,' you should forgive him."

LUKE 17:1–4

PRAYER

Lord, you taught us that we should continue to forgive those who harm us. In my own life I hold on to old wrongs and grudges without thinking of your teaching. Help me in these Lenten days to put aside old grievances so that your love may grow ever stronger in my life.

LENTEN ACTION

Everyone knows stories of friends or families broken apart by old quarrels or mistakes from the past. If you have one of these in your life, think and pray seriously during this Lent about how to reconcile and forgive. If your life is free of these, thank God for the peace you enjoy and see if you can be a peacemaker for others.

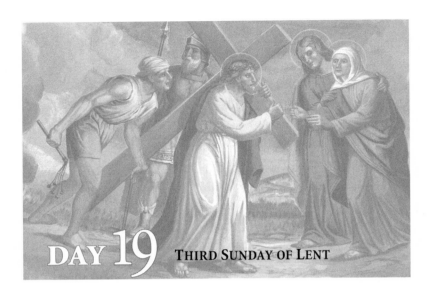

DAY 19   THIRD SUNDAY OF LENT

Doing God's Will

What reasons do we have...to give ourselves to God to adopt this holy practice of doing God's Will always and in all things? The first is drawn from the *Pater noster*,...may your will be done on earth as it is in heaven. Just as the angels and the blessed in heaven do incessantly his holy and adorable will, likewise our Lord, desiring that we do the same here on earth, wanted us to do it in the same way and with the greatest perfection possible, etc.

"CONFORMITY TO THE WILL OF GOD," CONFERENCE 142

How to Pray

This is how you are to pray: Our Father in heaven, hallowed be your name, your kingdom come, your will be done, on earth as in heaven. Give us today our daily bread; and forgive us our debts, as we forgive our debtors; and do not subject us to the final test, but deliver us from the evil one.

MATTHEW 6:9–13

Prayer

God, our Father, I turn to you so often in prayer in the words that Jesus gave us. During this Lent, may I probe more deeply into these words and learn to seek out your will for me and to do it always.

Lenten Action

Take the Lord's Prayer in any of its versions in the gospels and write it out slowly and meditatively. Think in particular about the phrase "thy will be done." Apply it to yourself and examine where you believe the Lord's will is for you today.

Success in Jesus Alone

*N*o, Monsieur, neither philosophy, nor theology, nor discourses can act in souls; Jesus Christ must be involved in this with us—or we with Him—so that we may act in Him and He in us, that we may speak as He did and in His Spirit, as He Himself was in His Father, and preached the doctrine He had taught Him; those are the words of Holy Scripture.

"ADVICE TO ANTOINE DURAND," CONFERENCE 153

EMPTY ARGUMENTS

Let no one deceive you with empty arguments, for because of these things the wrath of God is coming upon the disobedient. So do not be associated with them. For you were once darkness, but now you are light in the Lord. Live as children of light.

EPHESIANS 5:6–8

PRAYER

Loving Lord, I want to do your will and live as you lived, but I fear doing so save on my own terms. Let me not hide behind empty words but rather imitate you in your self-giving love for others. Only then will I find my true rest in you.

LENTEN ACTION

Words well-spoken can ensnare a person. Take some time to examine your words spoken today. Were they meant to hurt or to heal? Were they full of yourself or the Spirit of Jesus? Make sure that your exterior life of prayer and piety matches your interior life. If the two do not coincide, try to probe why this is so. The goal is to live as a child of light.

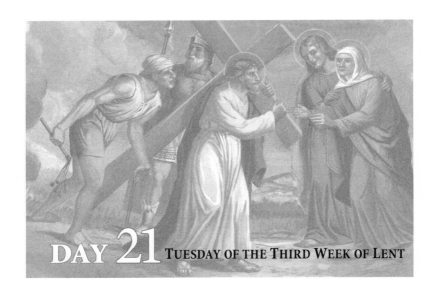

Little Attachments

*H*e said also that people, especially a Missioner, had to be constantly mortified, that we had to cut, prune, sever, and rid ourselves of the attachments we might have for little things— even for certain prayers—and that this was being an idolater of those particular objects.

"TRIALS AND ATTACHMENTS," CONFERENCE 89

THE THINGS OF A CHILD

When I was a child, I used to talk as a child, think as a child, reason as a child; when I became a man, I put aside childish things.

1 CORINTHIANS 13:11

PRAYER

God, almighty Father, I want to have you alone as the center of my life. Help me rid myself of all that is not of you, all attachments, all childish things. Fill me instead with yourself that I may come one day to live for you alone as your son Jesus did.

LENTEN ACTION

"Mortification" means putting something to death; in Lent, it can refer to annihilating everything in life that is not of God. Take a look around you and see what physical things you cannot live without. Ask yourself why this is so. Do you thus offer them the worship of idolatry? If they are at the center of your life, where is God? These questions can occupy an entire Lent.

Compassion

[Paul said:] I have made myself all to all, so that the complaint Our Lord formerly made through one of the Prophets, *Sustinui qui simul mecum contristaretur, et non fuit* doesn't fall on us: "I waited to see if someone would sympathize with me in my sufferings, and there was none." For that purpose, we have to try to stir our hearts to pity, make them sensitive to the sufferings and miseries of our neighbor, and ask God to give us the true spirit of mercy.

"THE SPIRIT OF MERCY AND COMPASSION," CONFERENCE 152

LIFE WITHOUT COMPASSION

You know my reproach, my shame, my disgrace; before you stand all my foes. Insult has broken my heart, and I am weak; I looked for compassion, but there was none, for comforters, but found none. Instead they put gall in my food; for my thirst they gave me vinegar.

PSALM 69:20–22

PRAYER

Lord, we praise you for your everlasting mercy. May I also learn mercy in my life through greater sensitivity to the pains and miseries of those around me. Open the eyes of my heart to my sisters and brothers in distress.

LENTEN ACTION

Pick out a story in the news today that involves the suffering and misery of others. Try to put yourself in their place to fathom what has just happened in their lives. Use this imaginative contact with others to then reach out to someone close to you and be the bearer of the mercy and compassion of God toward him. Sometimes even the simplest word or gesture can flood a soul with relief.

Pompous Preaching

Go find me something similar in that affected delivery, in that great pomp, and amid that vain display of eloquence; find me something similar. Very rarely do we see a single person converted by such preaching in the course of Advent and Lent year after year. We observe this in Paris. What restitution do we see from all those eloquent sermons? Do you see a large number of conversions, Messieurs? Alas, it would be hard to find one, a single one!

"METHOD TO BE FOLLOWED IN PREACHING," CONFERENCE 133

Babbling Like Pagans

Let your "Yes" mean "Yes," and your "No" mean "No." Anything more is from the evil one.

Matthew 5:37

In praying, do not babble like the pagans, who think that they will be heard because of their many words. Do not be like them. Your Father knows what you need before you ask him.

Matthew 6:5–8

Prayer

Lord, let the simplicity that you taught and practiced be my guide. Help me avoid in my prayer useless repetitions and words said only out of routine, and make my words flow from a heart totally given to you.

Lenten Action

Vincent de Paul was an acute observer of the people of his time, and he understood how religion was often only superficial. Think today about your own religious practices and pray for the light to see whether any of them are performed just superficially or out of routine. Do what you can for at least one of them to become more simple and earnest in prayer.

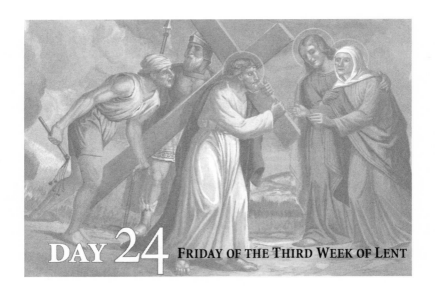

Study and Learning

We have to study in such a way that love corresponds to knowledge, especially for those studying theology, and do it in the manner of Cardinal de Berulle, who, as soon as he had grasped a truth, gave himself to God either to practice a certain thing, to enter into certain sentiments, or to produce acts; and by this means, he acquired a holiness and learning so solid that anything similar could scarcely be found.

"REPETITION OF PRAYER," CONFERENCE 98

STUDY GOD'S WORD

How I love your law, Lord! I study it all day long. Your commandment makes me wiser than my foes, as it is forever with me. I have more insight than all my teachers, because I ponder your testimonies.

PSALM 119:97–99

PRAYER

Heavenly Father, we have your word spread out before us in loving profusion in the holy Scriptures. As I listen to your word proclaimed and as I study it, may it take root in my heart and transform me. Give me an ever-deeper delight in your teachings.

LENTEN ACTION

Even if you do not have a well-worn copy of the Scriptures, particularly the New Testament, make this Lent a time for reading and study of God's word in the Bible. Pick a passage, such as the gospel of the day's liturgy, and read it slowly and meditatively. Doing so with others in a Bible study group can be a great help to grow in this practice.

Prayer for Priests

*M*y Savior, all [speaking] will be useless, if you don't put your hand to it; your grace has to actualize all that was said in order to give us that spirit without which we can do nothing. O Lord, give us the spirit of your priesthood, which your Apostles and the first priests who followed them had; give us the true spirit of this sacred character....For we, too, are only weak people, Lord, poor workers and peasants.

"THE ECCLESIASTICAL STATE" CONFERENCE 141

PRIESTLY VIRTUES

But you, man of God,...pursue righteousness, devotion, faith, love, patience, and gentleness. Compete well for the faith. Lay hold of eternal life, to which you were called when you made the noble confession in the presence of many witnesses.

1 TIMOTHY 6:11–12

PRAYER

Lord Jesus, at the Last Supper you established the priesthood in your Church. Grant to those whom you have called to this office the spirit of the great and holy priests who have served your people everywhere in all ages. Heal what is broken and let the light of your word shine forth in their ministry.

LENTEN ACTION

So much has happened in today's Church that tends to diminish the priesthood. Take a special time today to pray for those priests who minister to you. A word of praise or appreciation from you for their dedication will go a long way to strengthen them in their perseverance.

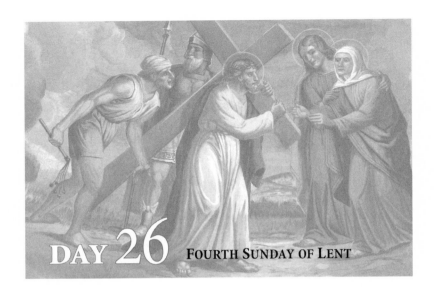

DAY 26   FOURTH SUNDAY OF LENT

Poverty

*O*h, if God were to grant us the grace of opening the curtain that prevents us from seeing such beauty [of poverty]; if only he were to lift, by his grace, all the veils that the world and our self-love cast before our eyes, messieurs, we'd be immediately delighted with the charms of that virtue which delighted the heart and affections of the Son of God! It was the virtue of the Son of God; he willed to have it as his own.

"POVERTY," CONFERENCE 132

POVERTY OF JESUS

As they were proceeding on their journey someone said to him, "I will follow you wherever you go." Jesus answered him, "Foxes have dens and birds of the sky have nests, but the Son of Man has nowhere to rest his head."

LUKE 9:57–58

PRAYER

Lord Jesus, I cannot follow you in your physical poverty, but I wish to follow you in the rejection that I must make of all that is not of you. By your grace may I see the beauty of living only for you, even at the cost of putting aside the comforts and leisure time I so crave.

LENTEN ACTION

One aspect of Lenten fasting is to excise from our lives those things that compromise our commitments to the gospel. This discipline is also a regular part of Christian life, not limited to Lent. Pray over the poverty of Jesus and focus on at least one aspect of your life that you could strip away in honor of that poverty. The result should be a greater capacity for love.

Humility Before Others

It's a good practice to get down to particulars in humbling matters, when prudence allows us to admit them openly, because of the benefit we draw from this, overcoming our repugnance to reveal what pride might want to keep hidden. Saint Augustine himself made public the secret sins of his youth.

"HUMILITY," CONFERENCE 36

HUMILITY BEFORE GOD

The Pharisee took up his position and spoke this prayer to himself, "O God, I thank you that I am not like the rest of humanity—greedy, dishonest, adulterous—or even like this tax collector. I fast twice a week, and I pay tithes on my whole income." But the tax collector stood off at a distance and would not even raise his eyes to heaven but beat his breast and prayed, "O God, be merciful to me a sinner."

LUKE 18:11–13

PRAYER

Father, I dislike the Pharisee of the gospel, but I often see myself doing exactly what he did. Fill me with the courage to see myself as I truly am, with both good and evil. May I praise you for the good accomplished by your will, and, for the evil, I beg your mercy.

LENTEN ACTION

We learned from our earliest days that "humility is truth." During this Lent, take time to look inside yourself, your truest self. Accept what you see in all humility. Talking about blessings and failures with a friend or confidant can be exactly the impetus you need to admit the truth about yourself.

Freedom From Possessions

*B*ut this strong desire to have possessions made [Judas] grumble against his companions; he begrudged them everything; he even became angry with persons who tried to honor his master by their generous gifts, because the gifts didn't go into his purse; he feathered his own nest; he stole the money of the community and of the poor. What else? He even regretted what was spent on the Son of God....This vice, like others, slips in imperceptibly.

"POVERTY," CONFERENCE 132

JUDAS, A THIEF

Then Judas the Iscariot, one (of) his disciples, and the one who would betray him, said, "Why was this oil not sold for three hundred days' wages and given to the poor?" He said this not because he cared about the poor but because he was a thief and held the money bag and used to steal the contributions.

JOHN 12: 4–6

PRAYER

Lord, you opened the eyes of the blind and gave them new sight. I bring my blindness to you today and beg you for the sight I need. With it, help me to see what it is that I truly need in this world and to rid myself of anything that isn't of you.

LENTEN ACTION

Spring cleaning is a great custom, coming as it does during Lent. This season, ask for open eyes to see whatever it is in your life that does not belong there and then to rid yourself of it. The sacrament of reconciliation, confession, can be a good beginning. As a symbol of your determination, resolve to clean out a box or a drawer filled with useless items. Holding on to what is useless or outdated is a sort of theft that keeps us comfortable.

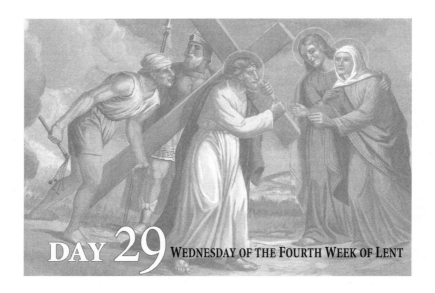

Gentleness, the Virtue

*S*ometimes we see people who seem to be endowed with great gentleness, which, however, is very often only a result of their natural moderation. They don't, however, have Christian gentleness, whose characteristic is to repress and stifle the sallies of the contrary vice.

"GENTLENESS," CONFERENCE 44

LOVE IS GENTLE

Love is patient, love is kind. It is not jealous, (love) is not pomp-
ous, it is not inflated, it is not rude, it does not seek its own
interests, it is not quick-tempered, it does not brood over injury,
it does not rejoice over wrongdoing but rejoices with the truth.

1 CORINTHIANS 13:4–6

PRAYER

Lord Jesus, Vincent de Paul tried to imitate your gentleness, which he saw as a great need in his life. Help me, through a meditative reading of your holy word, to put on your spirit of gentleness in my own life and to leave aside all anger and harshness.

LENTEN ACTION

Lent is a time to consider growth in virtue, that is, a particular strength of the spirit that we can see in the life of Jesus. Ask yourself in your own quiet time which strength of spirit you need. For many, it is gentleness. If you find anger and harshness breaking out in unexpected ways, offer these moments to the Lord as a witness of your need and beg forgiveness from him and from others you may have offended.

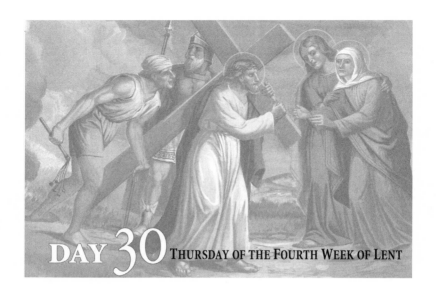

Priesthood

*W*hat a great thing a good priest is! What is there that a good priest can't do and what conversions can he not obtain?

"FORMATION OF THE CLERGY," CONFERENCE 4

WITNESSES TO THE PASSION, DEATH AND RESURRECTION

We are witnesses of all that he did both in the country of the Jews and (in) Jerusalem. They put him to death by hanging him on a tree. This man God raised (on) the third day and granted that he be visible...to us, the witnesses chosen by God in advance.... He commissioned us to preach to the people and testify that he is the one appointed by God as judge of the living and the dead.

ACTS 10:39–42

PRAYER

Lord Jesus, you formed your first disciples to be the priests of your Church. You confided to them the continuation of your mission, the forgiveness of sins, and the salvation of souls. Strengthen the priests of your Church and bless their endeavors for your people.

LENTEN ACTION

On the Thursdays of Lent, the Church remembers the Last Supper with the institution of the sacraments of the Eucharist and Holy Orders. The next time you go to Mass, thank God for the priests who have been part of your life. Look for an occasion, likewise, to thank the priests and deacons who minister to you.

Mutual Forgiveness

I hope from your goodness and infinite generosity that you'll forgive me this immense debt, as you did for the poor debtor in the gospel, *Et omne debitum dimisi ei* (Matthew 18:32), because your mercy and goodness are infinitely greater than my unworthiness and malice.

"EXHORTATION TO A DYING BROTHER," CONFERENCE 102

Forgiving the Neighbor

His master summoned him and said to him, "You wicked servant! I forgave you your entire debt because you begged me to. Should you not have had pity on your fellow servant, as I had pity on you?"

MATTHEW 18:32–33

Prayer

Lord, let me never forget your mercy toward me. At the same time, strengthen me to offer that same mercy and forgiveness to those who have ever offended me in any way. I lift them all up to you today, begging your mercy and the healing of my wounds.

Lenten Action

Take some time today to review any hurt that you suffered, either recently or long ago. Ask in prayer for healing for yourself and then for the one who hurt you. If you have never been reconciled and you still could be, ask what is holding you back. Read the whole parable in Matthew 18 about forgiveness and see how it applies in your case.

Blessings on Mustard Seeds

$\mathcal{T}$he topic of their discussion was what should be done to spend the time of Lent in a holy manner....You see, then, brothers, how God hides treasures in things that seem so ordinary, and in the slightest details of the truths and mysteries of our religion. They're like tiny mustard seeds that produce huge trees when our Lord is pleased to shed His blessings on them.

"MEDITATION," CONFERENCE 71

PARABLE OF THE MUSTARD SEED

He proposed another parable to them. "The kingdom of heaven is like a mustard seed that a person took and sowed in a field. It is the smallest of all the seeds, yet when full-grown it is the largest of plants. It becomes a large bush, and the 'birds of the sky come and dwell in its branches.'"

MATTHEW 13:31–32

PRAYER

God of all creation, you have filled our world with beauty and light. During this Lent, may my senses be opened to your presence all about me, from seeds to trees, in life in all its forms. In seeing you there, may I know more profoundly that your love toward me is everlasting.

LENTEN ACTION

Plant a seed or a spring bulb during Lent and watch it grow. As it comes forth, see the loving hand of God there, even in these most ordinary but marvelous signs of life. Take pleasure in new life all about you.

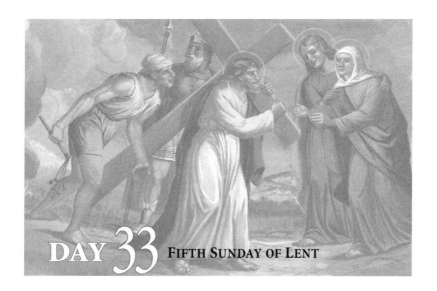

Complacency

*H*umility should incline you also to avoid all self-satisfaction, which slips mainly into works that have some glory in them. O Monsieur, how dangerous to good works is the venom of vain complacency! It's a plague that corrupts the holiest actions and soon causes us to forget God. In the name of God, be on your guard against this failing, since it's one of the things that presents the greatest danger I know to advancement in the spiritual life and perfection.

"ADVICE TO ANTOINE DURAND," CONFERENCE 153

OVERCONFIDENCE

Tremble, you who are so complacent! Shudder, you who are so confident! Strip yourselves bare, with only a loincloth for cover. Beat your breasts for the pleasant fields, for the fruitful vine. For the soil of my people, overgrown with thorns and briers. For all the joyful houses, the exultant city.

ISAIAH 32:11–13

PRAYER

Almighty Father, you alone are great and to you alone belongs the glory. May any good that I see in myself be tempered by understanding the danger I run of being complacent in my life. Sin is always present and can easily overtake me. Help me to place my entire life in your caring hands.

LENTEN ACTION

The prophet Isaiah saw the complacency of the people of his time, happy and content for the work of their own hands. Think of your own successes in life, with family, education, career, and relationships. Do you bow down in worship to yourself, or do you find your center in God alone? Pray for the strength you need for this continuous conversion.

The Aim of Life

*I*s there anyone better suited or more in conformity with God's plan than persons who have emptied themselves of self and have no other aim than to use their lives for the glory of His divine majesty and the salvation of the neighbor?

"REPETITION OF PRAYER," CONFERENCE 146

LEAST OF THE APOSTLES

Last of all, as to one born abnormally, he appeared to me. For I am the least of the apostles, not fit to be called an apostle, because I persecuted the church of God. But by the grace of God I am what I am, and his grace to me has not been ineffective. Indeed, I have toiled harder than all of them; not I, however, but the grace of God (that is) with me.

1 CORINTHIANS 15:8–10

PRAYER

Lord, even the great Apostle Paul, who had persecuted your church, emptied himself through conversion to your way. Like him, may I increasingly be converted to your way through the action of your grace in my life. All glory be to you.

LENTEN ACTION

Asking yourself the same question that Saint Vincent asked, examine your own ordinary and daily life to see whether your basic aim in life is to use your life for God's glory and the salvation of the neighbor. Lent is the right time to ask such penetrating questions about eternal truths.

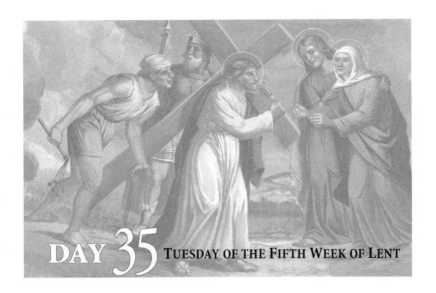

Mortification, Doing God's Will

*W*ho renounces himself more than the person who never does his own will but always that of God? And who mortifies himself more? And if, on the other hand, it's said in Holy Scripture that the person who remains faithful to God is made one spirit with him, who remains more faithful to God...than the man who never does anything but the will of the same God, and never his own...?

"REPETITION OF PRAYER," CONFERENCE 143

JOINED IN SPIRIT TO JESUS

God raised the Lord and will also raise us by his power. Do you not know that your bodies are members of Christ? ...Whoever is joined to the Lord becomes one spirit with him.

1 CORINTHIANS 6:14–15, 17

PRAYER

Lord Jesus, through my baptism I have become joined to you. May I grow during this Lent in a deeper sense of true identity as a baptized person. Help me put aside all that does not contribute to this new life. Send me your Holy Spirit for my strength.

LENTEN ACTION

The goal of the Lenten fast and abstinence is not to suffer but to be purified, and not just in the body but mainly in the spirit. Take another look today at the goal of your Lenten observances and try to pinpoint where the greatest purification in your life needs to happen. Saint Vincent pointed to doing God's will as the heart of this issue.

True Virtue

*I*f the man who directs and forms others and speaks to them is animated with only a human spirit, those who see him, listen to him, and strive to imitate him will become totally human: no matter what he says and does, he'll inspire them with only the appearance of virtue, and not the substance.

"ADVICE TO ANTOINE DURAND," CONFERENCE 153

PUT ON THE LORD JESUS CHRIST

It is the hour now for you to awake from sleep. For our salvation is nearer now than when we first believed; the night is advanced, the day is at hand. Let us then throw off the works of darkness (and) put on the armor of light; …But put on the Lord Jesus Christ, and make no provision for the desires of the flesh.

ROMANS 13:11–12, 14

PRAYER

God of the day and of light, praise be to you for the brightness of Jesus. In my baptism I was joined to him in a new life. May this life also be full of light for all those whom I meet. May I never inspire darkness in them.

LENTEN ACTION

Today, reflect on your baptism and on its continued meaning in your life. Does it mean anything to you? Is it transformative? One way to celebrate the sacrament is to commemorate the anniversary of your baptism. Do you know the date? If not, either look for it or pick another that can speak to you of when you first "put on the Lord Jesus Christ."

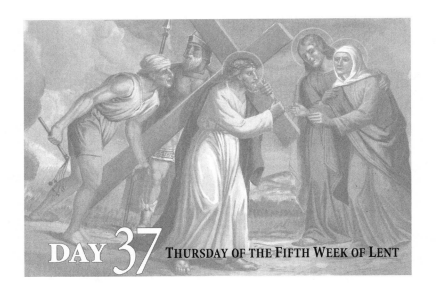

Reconciliation

ost of (the parishioners) were unwilling even to hear Mass, and would leave the church when they saw (their pastor) go to the altar. In a word, it was a very bad situation, and I've yet to see anything like it. They swore they'd never go to confession to him and that they'd rather let Easter go by without receiving Communion.

"RECONCILIATION," CONFERENCE 3

BE RECONCILED

> *Therefore, if you bring your gift to the altar, and there recall that your brother has anything against you, leave your gift there at the altar, go first and be reconciled with your brother, and then come and offer your gift.*

MATTHEW 5:23–24

PRAYER

Father of all, I am often asked to share a sign of your peace and reconciliation at Mass. Help me to make this gesture truly genuine and heartfelt. May it also remind me to be at peace with others who are not present with me in church. Only your Spirit can strengthen me for the difficult relationships I encounter.

LENTEN ACTION

The ancient rite of sharing the peace before receiving holy Communion has its roots in the gospel. During the season of Lent try to focus on its inner meaning each time. A special smile or word of peace is an added gift to the person to whom you turn.

Love of Possessions

This renunciation must also be interior and come from the heart. Along with our possessions, we must also give up the attachment and love of possessions, and have no love for the perishable goods of this world. It's doing nothing, it's making a mockery of an exterior renunciation of goods, if we hold on to the desire to have them. God asks primarily for our heart—our heart—and that's what counts.

"POVERTY," CONFERENCE 132

NEW HEARTS

I will sprinkle clean water over you to make you clean; from all your impurities and from all your idols I will cleanse you. I will give you a new heart, and a new spirit I will put within you. I will remove the heart of stone from your flesh and give you a heart of flesh. I will put my spirit within you so that you walk in my statutes, observe my ordinances, and keep them.

EZEKIEL 36:25–27

PRAYER

Creator God, I sense so many needs in my life, but many of them are nothing in comparison with the need I have for you. As I move through this Lent and approach Easter, fill me with deeper love for you, for your people, especially those most abandoned.

LENTEN ACTION

Find a quiet time to sit and relax so as to feel your heart beating. Reread the passage from Ezekiel the prophet concerning stony hearts and natural hearts, and enter into the spirit of the Lenten season, when the Lord is asking for renewed, warm, and adaptable hearts.

God's Plan

*E*ternal Father, you have sent your Son to enlighten and teach everyone, and yet He appears to us something less than that! But wait a little, and you'll see God's plan; and because He determined not to allow the world to be lost and had compassion on it, that same Son will give His life for us.

"REPETITION OF PRAYER," CONFERENCE 160

A Carpenter's Son?

He came to his native place and taught the people in their synagogue. They were astonished and said, "Where did this man get such wisdom and mighty deeds? Is he not the carpenter's son? Is not his mother named Mary and his brothers James, Joseph, Simon, and Judas? Are not his sisters all with us? Where did this man get all this?" And they took offense at him.

MATTHEW 13:54–57

Prayer

Lord Jesus, the Church follows your life through the liturgical year. We see you as baby, a youth in the Temple, and a simple carpenter's son. Now, as we approach the holy days of your life-giving death and rising, we see your Father sending you for our salvation. Praise be to you for your life and the salvation offered to us.

Lenten Action

One problem with the liturgical year is that it can become routine. This year, prepare for the great days of Holy Week and Easter by rereading the passion narratives of each of the four gospels. Meditate on the realities proclaimed there and pick out one passage or verse that has special appeal to you at this time. Use that for prayer during the next several days.

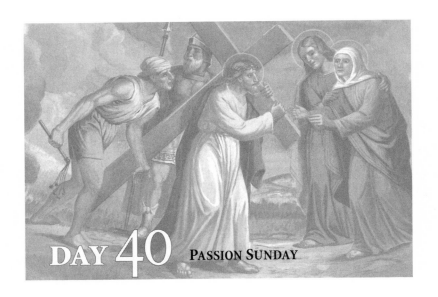

Transfigured With Pain

*Y*ou also see Him, radiant with splendor on Mount Tabor, and then, after that, you see Him cruelly treated, mocked, insulted, and scourged....We mustn't be surprised at seeing these changes in ourselves; but what we have to do is to thank God equally for one and the other state in which it will please His Divine Majesty that we may be—whether joy and consolation, or sadness and distress—and to love all the states in which God is pleased to place us, whatever they may be.

"REPETITION OF PRAYER," CONFERENCE 158

MOCKED AND SCOURGED

Then they spat in his face and struck him, while some slapped him, saying, "Prophesy for us, Messiah: who is it that struck you?" Then he released Barabbas to them, but after he had Jesus scourged, he handed him over to be crucified.

MATTHEW 26:67–68; 27:26

PRAYER

Heavenly Father, you made me full of light and darkness, joy and anguish. As I meditate on the joys and sufferings of Jesus your Son during this Holy Week, give me the faith I need to confide all my future into your loving hands. Help me to accept myself as I am, and to praise you for my creation.

LENTEN ACTION

As Good Friday approaches, meditate again on the crucifixion. Look intently at your crucifix and ponder the lights and darkness there. Move with Jesus from the glory of the transfiguration through the sorrow of the passion to the glory of the resurrection.

Prayer Without Action

*T*here are many who, recollected exteriorly, and filled with lofty sentiments of God interiorly, stop at that, and when it comes to the point of doing something, and they have the opportunity to act, they come up short.

"LOVE OF GOD," CONFERENCE 25

GARDEN OF OLIVES

Then they came to a place named Gethsemane, and he said to his disciples, "Sit here while I pray." He advanced a little and fell to the ground and prayed that if it were possible the hour might pass by him; he said, "Abba, Father, all things are possible to you. Take this cup away from me, but not what I will but what you will."

MARK 14:32, 35–36

PRAYER

Lord Jesus, in the Garden of Olives you were overtaken by sentiments of fear and abandonment. Give us as we pray a sense of your love for us which led from fear to the sacrifice of the Cross. May our prayer never be directed inwardly, focused on ourselves, but outwardly, on the growth of your kingdom.

LENTEN ACTION

Take the crucifix in your hands once again and look at it intently. Try to consider what the crucifixion meant, and how the Lord overcame his fear, the bloody sweat in the Garden of Olives, and moved to the complete sacrifice of himself. What are the lessons you can draw for your own life?

Lost in Ministry

*F*urthermore, you must have recourse to God through meditation in order to preserve your soul in His fear and love; for, alas, Monsieur, I'm obliged to tell you—and you must know this—that people are often lost while contributing to the salvation of others. The person who forgets himself while being occupied with external things does well on his own account.

"ADVICE TO ANTOINE DURAND," CONFERENCE 153

RUN SO AS TO WIN

Do you not know that the runners in the stadium all run in the race, but only one wins the prize? Run so as to win. Every athlete exercises discipline in every way. They do it to win a perishable crown, but we an imperishable one. Thus I do not run aimlessly; I do not fight as if I were shadowboxing. No, I drive my body and train it, for fear that, after having preached to others, I myself should be disqualified.

1 CORINTHIANS 9:24–27

PRAYER

Lord Jesus, eternal priest, protect those whom you have called to your priesthood. May their words and actions reflect your words and actions alone and transform their lives more completely into yours. May I also persevere to the end in my baptismal commitments to you.

LENTEN ACTION

Lent is a period of discipline. Examine your own Lenten disciplines today now that Easter is close. How have you done so far? Has your focus moved from the external to the internal, from the superficial to the deep things of God? Pray for your perseverance and renewal in faith and the love of God.

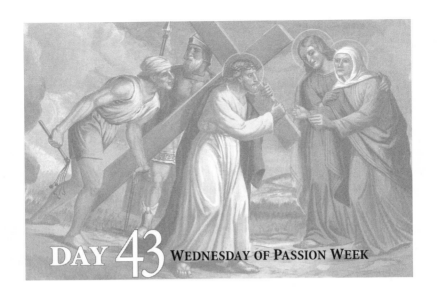

DAY 43 WEDNESDAY OF PASSION WEEK

To God Be the Glory

God makes use of whomever He pleases, of a wicked man as well as an upright one, even so far as to work miracles, as some hold that Judas did, he who betrayed Our Lord....Be careful to refer always to God all the glory of the good Our Lord will do for the Company in general or for each one of you and of the members that compose it in particular.

"ADMONITIONS," CONFERENCE 151

GLORY TO GOD

Now to him who can strengthen you, according to my gospel and the proclamation of Jesus Christ, according to the revelation of the mystery kept secret for long ages but now manifested through the prophetic writings and, according to the command of the eternal God, made known to all nations to bring about the obedience of faith, to the only wise God, through Jesus Christ be glory forever and ever. Amen.

ROMANS 16:25–27

PRAYER

Heavenly Lord, my tendency is to attribute the glory to myself and not to you. Help me during this Lent to put aside this tendency to blindness. Instead, may I see you everywhere and in all things and give the glory to you alone.

LENTEN ACTION

The prayers we say often can be overlooked for their content. Today, concentrate on the Doxology, or prayer of praise, to the holy Trinity. Say it and repeat it, thinking through its meaning. Think also of its opposite: "Glory be to me," and work to banish this perversion from your life. The goal is to seek and find God everywhere.

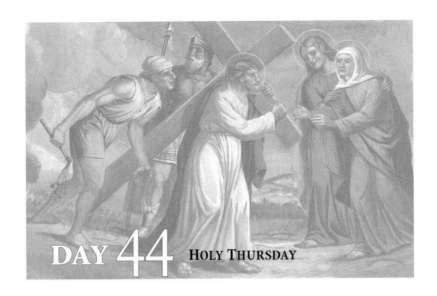

Inventive to Infinity

*F*urthermore, since love is inventive to infinity,...foreseeing that His absence could cause some forgetfulness or cooling off in our hearts, He wanted to avoid this danger by instituting the Most August Sacrament, in which He is as truly and substantially present as He is in heaven above.

"EXHORTATION TO A DYING BROTHER," CONFERENCE 102

EUCHARIST

For I received from the Lord what I also handed on to you, that the Lord Jesus, on the night he was handed over, took bread, and, after he had given thanks, broke it and said, "This is my body that is for you. Do this in remembrance of me." ...A person should examine himself, and so eat the bread and drink the cup.

1 CORINTHIANS 11:23–24, 28

PRAYER

Lord Jesus Christ, on this Holy Thursday, when you ate your paschal meal with your disciples, you instituted the sacraments of the Eucharist and priesthood. Fill me with an ever-greater sense of your presence and thus keep my devotion fresh and current in memory.

LENTEN ACTION

Try to participate as fully as possible in the ceremonies of Holy Thursday, with the washing of the feet in imitation of the loving action of Jesus. Receive holy Communion with great awareness of God's love inventive to infinity, and stay behind to pray at the altar where the blessed sacrament is enshrined.

Empty Yet Full

*F*or, take my word for it,...it's an infallible maxim of Jesus Christ,...that, as soon as a heart is empty of self, God fills it. God remains and acts in it; and it's the desire for shame that empties us of ourselves; that's humility, holy humility.

"THE ECCLESIASTICAL STATE," CONFERENCE 141

The Empty Heart of Jesus

But when they came to Jesus and saw that he was already dead, they did not break his legs, but one soldier thrust his lance into his side, and immediately blood and water flowed out. An eyewitness has testified, and his testimony is true; he knows that he is speaking the truth, so that you also may (come to) believe. For this happened so that the scripture passage might be fulfilled: "Not a bone of it will be broken." And again another passage says: "They will look upon him whom they have pierced."

JOHN 19:33–37

Prayer

Lord Jesus, I see in your wounded side and emptied heart a call to empty my own heart of myself. I often place myself at the center of my life, taking the place that rightfully belongs to you. Strengthen my attempts to humble myself, and fill me with yourself.

Lenten Action

The Sacred Heart of Jesus is so common a Catholic symbol as to be easily overlooked. Turn to a picture or statue of Jesus showing his heart and "look upon him," seeing in this sign of his love an invitation to turn your heart, full of self, into his.

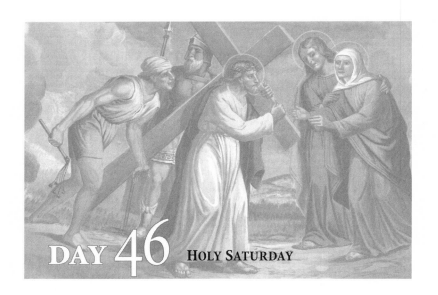

Baptismal Promises

*W*ould you want now to break your promise and go back on your word, which men of the world keep so religiously, and without which a man isn't a man? Yes, a man who doesn't keep his word isn't a man, he has only the appearance of one, but he's an animal, a wild animal, that deserves to be driven from the society of men.

"POVERTY," CONFERENCE 131

REPENT AND BE BAPTIZED

They asked Peter and the other apostles, "What are we to do, my brothers?" Peter (said) to them, "Repent and be baptized, every one of you, in the name of Jesus Christ for the forgiveness of your sins; and you will receive the gift of the holy Spirit. For the promise is made to you and to your children and to all those far off, whomever the Lord our God will call."

ACTS 2:37–39

PRAYER

Risen Lord, with the Church I celebrate your rising, singing Alleluia, and receiving the sacraments. I praise you for those reborn in baptism at this time, and I beg for a renewal of my own baptismal commitments. Thank you for holding me in your love; may I never fall away from you.

LENTEN ACTION

Do something special today to celebrate the feast of Easter, but take time to reflect on its inner and continuing meaning in your own life. Make your outward joy at Easter be a sign of your inward commitments to the Lord.

PART II

~~~~~

READINGS
for
EASTER

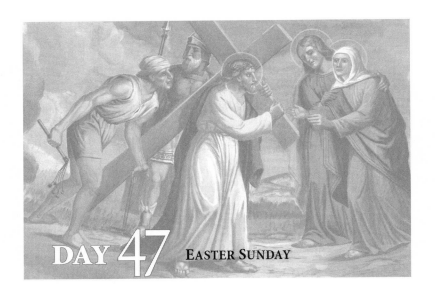

DAY 47   EASTER SUNDAY

Divine Mercy

They practice mercy, that beautiful virtue of which it's said, "Mercy is the distinctive feature of God." We practice it, too, and must do so all our lives: corporal mercy, spiritual mercy, mercy in the rural areas and in the missions by hastening to meet the needs of our neighbor.

"REPETITION OF PRAYER," CONFERENCE 157

MIGHTY DEEDS, WONDERS, AND SIGNS

Jesus the Nazorean was a man commended to you by God with mighty deeds, wonders, and signs, which God worked through him in your midst, as you yourselves know. This man, delivered up by the set plan and foreknowledge of God, you killed, using lawless men to crucify him. But God raised him up, releasing him from the throes of death, because it was impossible for him to be held by it.

ACTS 2:22–24

PRAYER

Almighty God, on this Easter day I bow in adoration of your mercy toward your people, and toward me in particular. In celebration of your love, may I devote myself to imitating your mercy in my daily life.

EASTER ACTION

Amid the Easter flowers, the glorious music, and the Alleluias, look again at your commitment to practicing the mercy of God, both corporal and spiritual. This will help to anchor your celebration in the realities of life.

Imitation of Jesus

*A*cknowledging that our life comes from His generous hand, we'd certainly commit an injustice if we refused to use it and to consume it according to His plans, in imitation of His Son Our Lord.

"THE SERVICE OF GOD," CONFERENCE 31

PAUL, IMITATOR OF CHRIST

Be imitators of me, as I am of Christ. I praise you because you remember me in everything and hold fast to the traditions, just as I handed them on to you.

PRAYER

Heavenly Father, during this week of Easter, strengthen my resolve always to see my life as a participation and imitation of your Son's life, death, and rising. May my actions be his actions, may the reverses I experience in life be changed by his sufferings and death, and may my entire life be transformed by the anticipation of my own rising to new life, as he did.

EASTER ACTION

When life gets rough and disagreeable, as it inevitably does, can you see it as transformed by the sufferings and death of Jesus? Can you see the resurrection to come? Take time during this Easter week to review an especially difficult moment that you are experiencing and try to see it as a participation in the Lord's own sufferings. At the very least, sing an Alleluia of praise and thanks for the Christ-life that you lead.

Good Vocations

*L*ord, send Your Church good workers, but they should be really good ones; send good Missioners, men such as they should be, to work hard in Your vineyard; persons, my God, truly detached from themselves, their own ease, and worldly goods; they can be a smaller number, provided they're good. Grant Your Church this grace, Lord.

"REPETITION OF PRAYER," CONFERENCE 155

LABORERS ARE FEW

After this the Lord appointed seventy (-two) others whom he sent ahead of him in pairs to every town and place he intended to visit. He said to them, "The harvest is abundant but the laborers are few; so ask the master of the harvest to send out laborers for his harvest. Go on your way; behold, I am sending you like lambs among wolves.

LUKE 10:1–3

PRAYER

Lord, I make my own the prayer of Saint Vincent for vocations. Strengthen those whom you have called. May they spend their lives in the proclamation of your holy word and show the good example of a Christian life through their daily lives. Bless them and give them good people to be with them and encourage them.

EASTER ACTION

Jesus chose the Apostles to be his witnesses in the world. For them this entailed a martyr's death. Pray today and regularly for good vocations in the Church, witnesses to the resurrection of Jesus, and a new life of faith.

Reasonable Care

If He gives orders in the Gospel not to worry about tomorrow, that should be interpreted to mean not to be too anxious or concerned about worldly goods, and absolutely not to neglect the means of keeping ourselves alive and clothing ourselves; otherwise, there would be no point in sowing any seed.

"ADVICE TO ANTOINE DURAND," CONFERENCE 153

WHY BE ANXIOUS?

Can any of you by worrying add a single moment to your life-span? Why are you anxious about clothes? Learn from the way the wild flowers grow. They do not work or spin. But I tell you that not even Solomon in all his splendor was clothed like one of them. If God so clothes the grass of the field, which grows today and is thrown into the oven tomorrow, will he not much more provide for you, O you of little faith?

MATTHEW 6:27–30

PRAYER

Creator God, all times and seasons are in your hand, and you send the bounties of nature to us. Help me in this Easter season to put myself ever more confidently in your hands, to rest there. May I also use all the faculties you have granted me to grow in your love and to be of service to others.

EASTER ACTION

This is the time to look at the flowers and to marvel at their color and display. Endeavor to see God's creative love there. His creation also extends to the human body and all its faculties for growth and human creativity. As you contemplate God's creation, see where you can be creative today in some new way, especially toward those most in need of help and support.

All Are Different

We'll see humility in one, gentleness in another, charity toward the neighbor in this one, the love of God in that one, regularity and exactness in that other one, and patience and exact obedience in another. And who does all that? God. God is the one, my dear confreres, who acts in those persons—more in some, less in others, according as the power of the Spirit of the same God is communicated to them.

"REPETITION OF PRAYER," CONFERENCE 162

FREEDOM IN CREATION

But who indeed are you, a human being, to talk back to God? Will what is made say to its maker, "Why have you created me so?" Or does not the potter have a right over the clay, to make out of the same lump one vessel for a noble purpose and another for an ignoble one?

ROMANS 9:20–21

PRAYER

God, heavenly Father, as I celebrate your son's resurrection this week, I celebrate your love poured out in so many ways on my sisters and brothers everywhere. You freely created them out of love, you redeemed them out of love, and you endow them with graces for your Church, each one differently. Help me to see and venerate your love for them.

EASTER ACTION

Self-acceptance is one of the greatest tasks in human life. Take some time during this Easter week to strengthen your commitment to accept yourself as you are, with every plus and minus. God made you as you are. Offer yourself to him in service as his creature redeemed by the death and rising of Jesus.

Evangelizing

*T*o help souls get to paradise through instruction and suffering. Doesn't that come close to what Our Lord came to do? Not only did He not have a stone on which to lay His head, but He came and went from one place to another to win souls for God and, in the end, He died for them. He certainly could not have made us understand more clearly how dear they are to Him, nor convince us more effectively to spare nothing to instruct them with His teachings and bathe them in the fountains of His Precious Blood.

"VOCATION," CONFERENCE 1

He Has Sent Me

He came to Nazareth, where he had grown up, and went according to his custom into the synagogue on the sabbath day. He stood up to read and was handed a scroll of the prophet Isaiah. He unrolled the scroll and found the passage where it was written: "The Spirit of the Lord is upon me, because he has anointed me to bring glad tidings to the poor. He has sent me to proclaim liberty to captives and recovery of sight to the blind, to let the oppressed go free, and to proclaim a year acceptable to the Lord."

Luke 4:16–19

Prayer

God our Father, as you bring me to the end of this holy season with the Church, give me the light I need to see how I am imitating, and how I should imitate, the life of Jesus in my own life. May I be transformed into a more perfect reflection of his life as I live my own.

Easter Action

This Easter week is a meditative time given us to reflect on what we are actually called to do with our lives. The key for any Christian is to do what Jesus did. Take some devotional time today to examine one aspect of your life, especially where you spend the most time and energy. How does this reflect the life and activity of Jesus? Where could you reform the center of your life?

Our Lords and Masters

*C*ome then, my dear confreres, let's devote ourselves with re-newed love to serve persons who are poor, and even to seek out those who are the poorest and most abandoned; let's acknow-ledge before God that they're our lords and masters and that we're unworthy of rendering them our little services.

"LOVE FOR THE POOR," CONFERENCE 164

A FATHER TO THE NEEDY

For I rescued the poor who cried out for help, the orphans, and the unassisted; the blessing of those in extremity came upon me, and the heart of the widow I made joyful. I wore my honesty like a garment; justice was my robe and my turban. I was eyes to the blind, and feet to the lame was I; I was a father to the needy; the rights of the stranger I studied, and I broke the jaws of the wicked man; from his teeth I forced the prey.

JOB 29:12–17

PRAYER

Lord, you taught us that the poor are always with us. May I never avert my gaze or my love for the most abandoned, those who are, in Saint Vincent's words, our lords and masters. After the experience of Lent and Easter, may I now be purified in my love for all your people.

EASTER ACTION

In Easter week, strengthened by the discipline of Lent and the celebrations of Holy Week, determine what you can now do regularly in the future for the care of "our lords and masters," the abandoned and outcasts of society.

Years Well Spent

*A*las, what is our life, so quickly passing? For myself, I'm in my seventy-sixth year; yet, right now all that time seems almost like a dream to me; all those years have gone by. Ah, Messieurs, how fortunate are those who use every moment of their life in the service of God, and offer themselves unconditionally to Him! What consolation do you think they'll get from this at the end of their life?

"REPETITION OF PRAYER," CONFERENCE 157

ALL MANKIND IS GRASS

All flesh is grass, and all their loyalty like the flower of the field. The grass withers, the flower wilts, when the breath of the LORD blows upon it. Yes, the people is grass! The grass withers, the flower wilts, but the word of our God stands forever.

ISAIAH 40:6–8

PRAYER

Dear Lord, as my life moves along, I am ever more aware of my need of conversion. With the strength of your grace, in my last days I will be able to rest in the thought that I have done at least a little in your service. Surround me always with your presence.

EASTER ACTION

At the close of this season of Lent and Easter, thank the Lord for his gifts of light and strength during these days. Review your good resolutions and strive to put them into practice daily. When your days end, you will thus be able see that you have grown in God's love.

Other Books in This Series from Liguori Publications

Lent and Easter Wisdom from Saint Alphonsus Liguori

Lent and Easter Wisdom from Saint Benedict

Lent and Easter Wisdom from C.K. Chesterton

Lent and Easter Wisdom from Henri J.M. Nouwen

Lent and Easter Wisdom from Fulton J. Sheen

Lent and Easter Wisdom from Pope John Paul II

Lent and Easter Wisdom from Saint Francis and Saint Clare of Assisi

Lent and Easter Wisdom from Thomas Merton

Lent and Easter Wisdom from Saint Ignatius of Loyola